Life in the
AMERICAN COLONIES

By Kristen Rajczak

Gareth Stevens
Publishing

Please visit our website, www.garethstevens.com. For a free color catalog of all our high-quality books, call toll free 1-800-542-2595 or fax 1-877-542-2596.

Library of Congress Cataloging-in-Publication Data

Rajczak, Kristen.
 Life in the American colonies / Kristen Rajczak.
     p. cm. — (What you didn't know about history)
 Includes index.
 ISBN 978-1-4339-8435-8 (pbk.)
 ISBN 978-1-4339-8436-5 (6-pack)
 ISBN 978-1-4339-8434-1 (library binding)
 1. United States—Social life and customs—To 1775—Juvenile literature. I. Title.
 E162.R35 2013
 973.01—dc23
                                        2012022216

First Edition

Published in 2013 by
Gareth Stevens Publishing
111 East 14th Street, Suite 349
New York, NY 10003

Copyright © 2013 Gareth Stevens Publishing

Designer: Dan Hosek and Michael J. Flynn
Editor: Kristen Rajczak

Photo credits: Cover, pp. 1, 9, 11, 19 Hulton Archive/Getty Images; p. 7 Richard Schlecht/ National Geographic/Getty Images; p. 13 MPI/Archive Photos/Getty Images; p. 15 Fotosearch/Archive Photos/Getty Images; p. 17 Jeff Greenberg/Photolibrary/ Getty Images; p. 21 Dusan Zidar/Shutterstock.com.

Printed in the United States of America

CPSIA compliance information: Batch #CW13GS: For further information contact Gareth Stevens, New York, New York at 1-800-542-2595.

CONTENTS

Words in the glossary appear in **bold** type the first time they are used in the text.

THE MAKING OF A NATION

All those living in the 13 American **colonies** played a role in US history. Some were British citizens looking for a fresh start. Others hailed from the Netherlands, Sweden, and Spain. Still others were slaves brought over from western Africa.

Some colonists became fishermen in Massachusetts, **plantation** owners in South Carolina, and shopkeepers in Virginia. Their jobs, food, and **religion** differed from colony to colony. But together, the colonists helped create the American **culture** we know today.

Did You Know?

The British began trying to colonize North America in the 1580s. The Roanoke colony was the first of their settlements. However, all the colonists there disappeared!

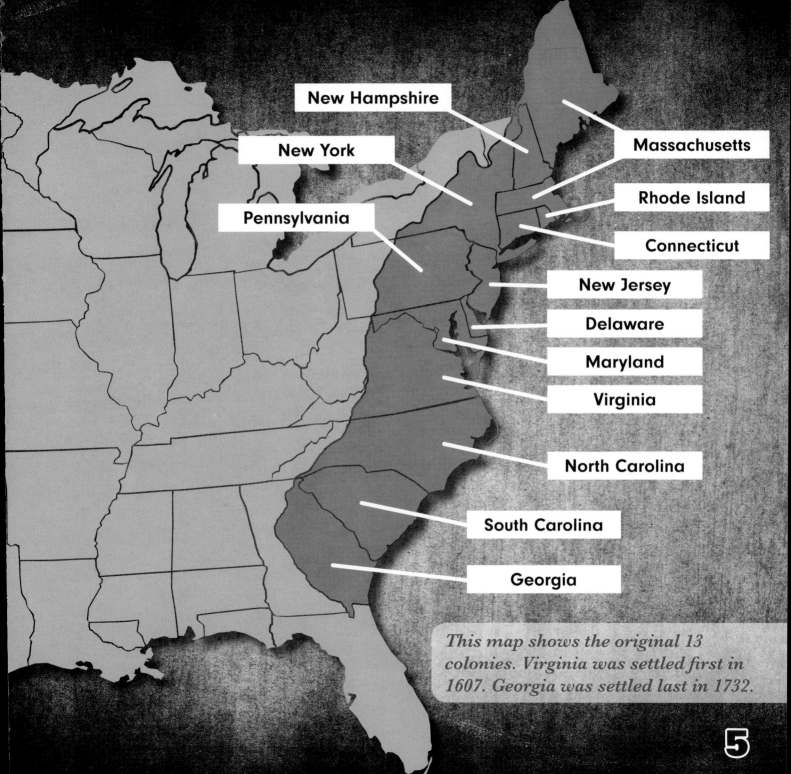

New Hampshire

New York

Pennsylvania

Massachusetts

Rhode Island

Connecticut

New Jersey

Delaware

Maryland

Virginia

North Carolina

South Carolina

Georgia

This map shows the original 13 colonies. Virginia was settled first in 1607. Georgia was settled last in 1732.

UNWILLING COLONISTS

Not all people living in the 13 colonies came by choice. Criminals from England were often shipped to the colonies to work instead of being put to death for their crimes. Children were sometimes kidnapped and brought to the colonies, too!

Large populations of indentured servants also came to the colonies. "Indentured" means they worked for a certain number of years in exchange for the cost of their passage. Some indentured servants found this arrangement fair. Others had been forced into it.

Did You Know?

It was common for a colonial man to pay for a woman to be brought to the colonies to be his wife.

Some colonists called the use of indentured servants and the practice of buying wives "white slavery."

7

THE WAY OF SLAVERY

The first slaves in the colonies worked somewhat like indentured servants. After a few years of service, they were freed. But for much of the colonial period, slavery was legal and lifelong in every colony.

What slaves' lives were like depended on where they lived. Slaves working in homes or in cities often ate better and had nicer clothing than those working in a plantation's fields. Mostly women, these slaves often worked on Sundays, unlike most field slaves.

Did You Know?

Slaves came from tribes all over Africa, mainly those on the western coast. Their cultures were often as different from each other as the backgrounds of the European colonists.

The practice of selling slaves started early in colonial history. This picture shows slaves arriving in Virginia in 1619.

9

Many colonists traveled to America to escape religious **persecution**. Some colonies, such as Maryland, were even founded for followers of a certain faith. Even so, colonists still faced many problems when they arrived. They had to build homes and roads, and learn to grow food in unfamiliar surroundings.

The colonists also caught—and died from—new illnesses. They weren't prepared for hard New England winters and terribly hot summers in the South. Additionally, fear of Native American tribes rose as attacks occurred on the growing colonies.

Did You Know?
Before 1640, colonists often died before they'd been in America a year. One-fourth of babies didn't live to their first birthday.

It was common for colonists to fight with some Native American tribes and be friendly with others.

11

WORKING THE FARM

Colonists' lives in the northernmost colonies were often unlike those of colonists in the South because of **climate** differences. For example, farmers in New England only had a short season during which to grow and **harvest** crops. Plantation owners in the South could grow their "cash crops"—such as tobacco—almost year-round.

On both northern farms and southern plantations, though, workers were valuable. In England, there was little land and many workers to farm it. In the colonies, it was just the opposite.

Did You Know?

A few plantation owners had grand homes and hundreds of slaves. Most southern farmers didn't, though.

On small farms, colonial families worked together to harvest crops and take care of livestock.

13

TOWN AND COUNTRY

Communities in the 13 colonies were small in both the North and South. By the 1700s, only five communities were big enough to be called cities.

Poorly built roads made travel hard, and colonists often didn't leave their town, much less their colony. This separation led to many of the differences between colonial communities. Virginia had clear social classes, complete with an upper class "gentry" that held most of the power. Massachusetts, on the other hand, gave men more of a say.

Did You Know?

During the mid-1700s, colonial families commonly had six to eight children. However, every time a baby was born, families worried for the lives of the baby and mother.

Whether through town government or style of dress, all the colonies showed some connection to their British rulers.

GETTING DRESSED

Wealthier colonial families tried to keep up with clothing styles in England. That often meant ordering clothing from London that had been shipped there from all over the world! A lady could buy a silk gown made in China for herself and a shirt made in northern Europe for her father. These items might even be **tailored** especially for the person meant to wear them.

Other colonists didn't buy clothes. Women often wove their own cloth to sew into clothes for the family.

Did-You-Know?

Colonists wore "dress" clothing for fancier occasions, such as balls or parties. To be in their "undress" meant they were wearing everyday clothing.

Like us, colonists chose what to wear based on what they were doing. They wouldn't wear their best clothes to wash cookware!

17

 GOOD TIMES

Colonists had to work hard. But they made time for fun, too! The Puritans in Massachusetts had a weeklong Thanksgiving celebration. In New York, colonists liked to fish and went sledding and ice skating in the winter. Southern colonists loved to dance! Horse racing was also popular in the southern colonies.

In many colonies, especially those in New England, church services were a weekly social event. Town meetings were also good times to visit with friends and neighbors.

Did-You-Know?

In 1635, the first school in the colonies opened in Boston, Massachusetts.

Colonists' culture often played a big part in what they chose to do for fun.

BRITISH RULE

By the mid-1700s, all 13 American colonies were part of the British empire. Each colony had its own government headed by a governor who reported to the British king.

Many governors weren't concerned with the colonists' day-to-day lives and allowed many laws to pass. Some were pretty strange! During the 1620s, Virginia passed a law requiring the planting of mulberry trees. Silkworms had been brought to the colony in an effort to start a silk industry, and silkworms love mulberry trees!

Did-You-Know?
Even though the governor was in charge, colonists had a lot of freedom.

Food: Then and Now

What do you like to eat? Some of our favorite foods and drinks were enjoyed in the 13 colonies, too!

- The Dutch who settled in New York made waffles with wheat flour.

- Apples from trees brought over from England were used to make cider.

- Native Americans taught the colonists how to grow corn, which they made into breads, cereal, and even popcorn!

- Colonists drank coffee. But when they didn't have coffee beans, they ground up other seeds and beans, or herbs like chicory, to drink.

LOSSARY

climate: the average weather conditions of a place over a period of time

colony: a piece of land under the control of another country. Someone who lives in a colony is a colonist.

culture: the customs, practices, and beliefs of a group of people

harvest: to bring in a crop

persecution: the act of treating people who are different in a harmful way

plantation: a large farm

religion: a system of beliefs held by a group of people

tailor: to make clothing or make changes to clothing

FOR MORE INFORMATION

Books

Fisher, Verna. *Colonial Families.* White River Junction, VT: Nomad Press, 2011.

Raum, Elizabeth. *The Dreadful, Smelly Colonies: The Disgusting Details About Life During Colonial America.* Mankato, MN: Capstone Press, 2010.

Websites

Colonial Williamsburg Kids Zone
www.history.org/kids
Play games and explore activities that teach about life in colonial Williamsburg.

The 13 Colonies
www.socialstudiesforkids.com/graphics/13mapnew.htm
Use an interactive map to learn more about each of the 13 colonies.

INDEX